BOOST YOUR BRAIN

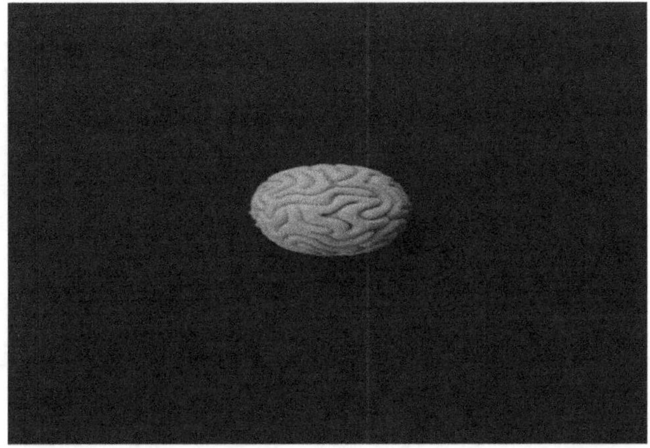

Enhance Your Cognitive Ability

Becky Brown

Table of contents

Introduction

In a bustling city where time seemed to move at an accelerated pace, Alex found themselves caught in the relentless whirlwind of daily life. Juggling work demands, social obligations, and the constant influx of information, their mind felt like a crowded highway during rush hour. The desire to boost their brain power became a compelling quest for clarity and cognitive vitality.

One day, while wandering through a quaint bookstore nestled between towering skyscrapers, Alex stumbled upon a dusty tome titled "MindMasters: Unleashing the Power Within." Intrigued, they flipped through its pages, discovering a trove of ancient wisdom, modern neuroscience, and practical techniques aimed at optimizing mental performance.

The journey to boost their brain had just begun. Alex embraced a holistic approach, delving into the secrets of a well-nourished mind and a balanced lifestyle. They explored the benefits of brain-boosting foods, incorporating omega-3-rich fish, antioxidant-packed berries, and nutrient-dense greens into their daily meals.

In tandem, mindfulness and meditation became pivotal practices in Alex's routine. Learning to quiet the mental chatter and focus on the present moment provided a sanctuary amidst the chaos. Guided by the book's insights, they embraced meditation as a powerful tool for enhancing cognitive abilities and fostering mental resilience.

As the days unfolded, Alex also discovered the art of lifelong learning. Engaging in stimulating activities, from picking up a musical instrument to mastering a new language, created neural connections that expanded their cognitive horizons. The once-static routine transformed into a dynamic dance of synapses firing with newfound vigor.

The journey to boost their brainpower not only enhanced Alex's cognitive abilities but also opened doors to creativity, resilience, and a profound sense of well-being. Armed with a revitalized mind, they navigated the urban jungle with newfound clarity, embracing each challenge as an opportunity to exercise their mental prowess.

In the pursuit of boosting their brain, Alex uncovered a profound truth – that the power to enhance one's mind lies

within, waiting to be unlocked by those

willing to embark on the transformative

journey of self-discovery.

Chapter one

What is Brain

The brain, a marvel of biological engineering, serves as the epicenter of human cognition, controlling every aspect of our thoughts, emotions, and actions. Nestled within the protective confines of the skull, this three-pound organ orchestrates an intricate symphony of neural connections that form the basis of our intelligence, memories, and consciousness.

Structure and Function:

At its core, the brain consists of billions of neurons, specialized cells that communicate with each other through electrochemical signals. These neurons form complex networks, creating the foundation for various cognitive functions. The brain is divided into distinct regions, each responsible for specific tasks. The cerebral cortex, for instance, governs advanced cognitive functions such as reasoning, language, and problem-solving, while the limbic system regulates emotions and memory.

Neurotransmitters:

Communication between neurons occurs through neurotransmitters, chemical messengers that traverse synapses – the tiny gaps between neurons. This intricate chemical dance ensures the seamless transmission of information, influencing mood, motivation, and overall cognitive function. Neurological and mental problems are associated with imbalances in neurotransmitter levels.

Plasticity and Adaptability:

One of the brain's most remarkable features is its plasticity – the ability to reorganize itself in response to experiences and environmental stimuli. This adaptability enables learning, memory formation, and recovery from injury. Neuroplasticity is particularly pronounced in early childhood but persists to a certain extent throughout life, allowing for ongoing growth and adaptation.

Cognition and Consciousness:

Cognition, the umbrella term for mental processes such as perception, attention, and problem-solving, relies on the intricate interplay of different brain regions. Consciousness, a philosophical

and scientific enigma, remains a
complex phenomenon rooted in the
brain's ability to integrate diverse
sensory inputs and generate
self-awareness.

Brain Health and Wellness:

For general well-being, maintaining
good brain health is essential.Factors
such as a balanced diet, regular
exercise, and sufficient sleep play
pivotal roles in supporting cognitive
function. Additionally, activities that
stimulate the brain, such as puzzles,
learning new skills, and social
interactions, contribute to cognitive

reserve and may help prevent cognitive decline.

Challenges and Disorders:

Despite its resilience, the brain is susceptible to various challenges. Neurological disorders like Alzheimer's disease, Parkinson's disease, and strokes can disrupt normal brain function. Mental health disorders, including depression, anxiety, and schizophrenia, also have profound impacts on the brain's intricate balance.

In conclusion, the brain stands as the ultimate command center of the human experience. Its complexity, adaptability, and vulnerability underscore the importance of nurturing and understanding this incredible organ for a life rich in cognitive vitality and emotional well-being.

Advancements in Neuroscience:

The relentless pursuit of understanding the brain has led to remarkable advancements in neuroscience. Cutting-edge technologies, such as functional magnetic resonance imaging (fMRI) and electroencephalography (EEG), provide unprecedented insights into the brain's activity in real-time.

These tools allow scientists to map neural circuits, observe changes during cognitive tasks, and explore the underlying mechanisms of various brain disorders.

Genetics and the Brain:

The study of genetics has unveiled a wealth of information about the genetic basis of brain development and function. Researchers explore the role of specific genes in neurological disorders, paving the way for targeted therapies. Genetic research also sheds light on individual differences in cognitive abilities and susceptibility to certain brain-related conditions.

Neurological Disorders and Treatments:

The understanding of neurological disorders has evolved, leading to improved diagnostic tools and innovative treatments. From pharmacological interventions to neurostimulation techniques, advancements in medical science offer hope for individuals affected by conditions such as epilepsy, multiple sclerosis, and traumatic brain injuries. Ongoing research aims to unravel the complexities of neurodegenerative diseases, with the ultimate goal of developing effective therapies.

Brain-Computer Interfaces (BCIs):

In the realm of futuristic possibilities, brain-computer interfaces (BCIs) stand out as a groundbreaking technology. BCIs facilitate direct communication between the brain and external devices, holding potential applications in restoring motor function for individuals with paralysis, enhancing cognitive abilities, and even merging human consciousness with artificial intelligence.

Ethical Considerations:

As neuroscience progresses, ethical considerations become paramount. The ability to manipulate and enhance cognitive functions raises questions about privacy, consent, and the potential for unintended consequences. Striking a balance between scientific exploration and ethical responsibility is crucial to navigating the uncharted territories of neuroscientific advancements.

The Brain and Beyond:

While the focus has traditionally been on the brain within the confines of the skull, emerging research explores the intricate connection between the brain and other bodily systems. The gut-brain axis, for instance, highlights the bidirectional communication between the digestive system and the brain, influencing mood, cognition, and overall well-being.

In the grand tapestry of human existence, the brain remains an awe-inspiring frontier. From the molecular intricacies of neurotransmission to the philosophical exploration of consciousness, the journey of understanding the brain is both a scientific endeavor and a profound exploration of what it means to be human. As neuroscience continues to unravel the mysteries of the brain, the

potential for enhancing cognitive

abilities, treating disorders, and pushing

the boundaries of human potential

beckons with promise and responsibility.

Chapter two

Brain Booster

Introduction to Brain Boosters:

Brain boosters, often referred to as nootropics or cognitive enhancers, are substances or activities designed to improve cognitive function, memory, creativity, and overall mental performance. The quest for enhanced mental capabilities has led to the exploration of various natural and synthetic compounds, as well as lifestyle strategies, that purportedly boost brain function.

1. Omega-3 Fatty Acids: Found in fatty fish like salmon, omega-3 fatty acids are crucial for brain health. They contribute to the structural integrity of brain cells and support cognitive function.

2. Antioxidants: Foods rich in antioxidants, such as berries and dark chocolate, help protect the brain from oxidative stress, potentially reducing the risk of cognitive decline.

3. Herbs and Adaptogens: Some herbs and adaptogens, like ginkgo biloba and rhodiola rosea, have

been traditionally used to support cognitive function and manage stress.

4. Caffeine: Found in coffee and tea, caffeine is a well-known stimulant that can temporarily enhance alertness and concentration.

Synthetic Brain Boosters:

1. Prescription Medications: Drugs like Modafinil and Adderall, prescribed for conditions like narcolepsy and ADHD, are sometimes used off-label as cognitive enhancers due to their stimulant effects.

2. Racetams: These synthetic
    compounds, including piracetam,
    are a class of nootropics that are
    believed to enhance memory and
    cognitive function. Their exact
    methods of action remain
    unknown, however.

3. Cholinergics: Compounds that
    influence the cholinergic system,
    such as choline and acetylcholine
    precursors, are thought to support
    memory and attention.

Lifestyle Strategies as Brain Boosters:

1. Regular Exercise: Physical activity
    has been linked to improved

cognitive function, including enhanced memory and increased neuroplasticity.

2. Adequate Sleep: Quality sleep is essential for cognitive performance, memory consolidation, and overall brain health.

3. Mental Stimulation: Engaging in intellectually stimulating activities, such as puzzles, learning new skills, or playing musical instruments, can promote cognitive reserve.

4. Healthy Diet: A well-balanced diet rich in nutrients, including antioxidants, omega-3 fatty acids,

and vitamins, supports brain
health.

Challenges and Considerations:

While the concept of brain boosters is
intriguing, it comes with challenges and
ethical considerations. The efficacy and
safety of many substances are still
under scrutiny, and the long-term effects
of some cognitive enhancers remain
unknown. Additionally, individual
responses to these boosters can vary,
highlighting the importance of
personalized approaches.

Conclusion:

In the pursuit of enhancing cognitive function, individuals often experiment with a combination of natural and synthetic brain boosters, along with lifestyle adjustments. It is essential to approach these interventions with caution, informed by scientific evidence and a consideration of potential risks. Ultimately, maintaining a healthy lifestyle that includes proper nutrition, exercise, and mental stimulation remains a cornerstone for optimal brain health and function.

Recipes for brain booster

Certainly! Here are a couple of recipes that incorporate ingredients known for their potential cognitive benefits:

1. **Berry and Nut Smoothie:**

Ingredients:

- 1 cup mixed berries (blueberries, strawberries, raspberries)
- 1 banana
- 1/2 cup Greek yogurt
- 1 tablespoon chia seeds
- 1 tablespoon flaxseeds
- 1/4 cup walnuts
- 1 cup spinach (optional)

- 1 cup almond milk

Instructions:

1. Blend the mixed berries, banana, Greek yogurt, chia seeds, flaxseeds, walnuts, and spinach (if using) until smooth.

2. Add almond milk gradually until you achieve your desired consistency.

3. Pour into a glass and enjoy this nutrient-packed smoothie, rich in antioxidants, omega-3 fatty acids, and vitamins.

2. Avocado and Salmon Salad:

Ingredients:

- 1 cup mixed salad greens (spinach, arugula, kale)
- 1/2 avocado, sliced
- 4 ounces smoked salmon, sliced
- 1/4 cup cherry tomatoes, halved
- 1/4 cup cucumber, sliced
- 1 tablespoon extra virgin olive oil
- 1 tablespoon lemon juice
- Salt and pepper to taste
- 1 tablespoon pumpkin seeds (optional)

Instructions:

1. In a large bowl, combine the salad
   greens, avocado slices, smoked
   salmon, cherry tomatoes, and
   cucumber.

2. In a small bowl, whisk together the
   olive oil, lemon juice, salt, and
   pepper to create the dressing.

3. Over the salad, drizzle with the
   dressing and toss lightly to mix.

4. Sprinkle pumpkin seeds on top if
   desired.

5. Serve this brain-boosting salad as
   a nutrient-dense lunch or dinner
   option, providing omega-3 fatty
   acids, antioxidants, and healthy
   fats.

3. Turmeric and Ginger Tea:

Ingredients:

- 1 teaspoon turmeric powder
- 1/2 teaspoon ginger, grated
- 1 tablespoon honey
- 1 tablespoon lemon juice
- 2 cups hot water

Instructions:

1. In a cup, combine turmeric powder, grated ginger, honey, and lemon juice.
2. Stir well after adding hot water to the mixture.

3. Give it a few minutes to steep.

4. Strain the tea to remove ginger particles.

5. Sip on this warm and comforting turmeric and ginger tea, known for its anti-inflammatory properties and potential cognitive benefits.

These recipes incorporate ingredients that are believed to support brain health, but it's essential to consult with a healthcare professional for personalized advice, especially if you have any dietary restrictions or health concerns.

4. Quinoa and Vegetable Stir-Fry:

Ingredients:

- 1 cup quinoa, cooked
- 1 tablespoon coconut oil
- 1 cup broccoli florets
- 1 bell pepper, thinly sliced
- 1 carrot, julienned
- 1 cup mushrooms, sliced
- 2 cloves garlic, minced
- 1 tablespoon soy sauce (low sodium)
- 1 teaspoon sesame oil
- 1 tablespoon fresh cilantro, chopped

- 1 tablespoon pumpkin seeds
  (optional)

Instructions:

1. Heat the coconut oil in a big skillet over medium heat.

2. Add garlic and sauté until fragrant.

3. Add broccoli, bell pepper, carrot, and mushrooms to the skillet. Stir-fry until vegetables are tender-crisp.

4. Mix the cooked quinoa well with the veggies.

5. In a small bowl, combine soy sauce and sesame oil. Pour over

the quinoa and vegetables,
tossing to coat evenly.

6. Garnish with fresh cilantro and
   pumpkin seeds if desired.

7. Enjoy this quinoa and vegetable
   stir-fry as a wholesome and
   brain-boosting meal, providing a
   mix of complex carbohydrates,
   fiber, and nutrients.

5. Dark Chocolate and Walnut Energy Bites:

Ingredients:

- 1 cup rolled oats

- 1/2 cup dark chocolate chips (70% cocoa or higher)
- 1/2 cup walnuts, chopped
- 1/2 cup almond butter
- 1/4 cup honey
- 1 teaspoon vanilla extract
- Pinch of sea salt

Instructions:

1. In a mixing bowl, combine rolled oats, dark chocolate chips, and chopped walnuts.
2. In a small saucepan, heat almond butter and honey over low heat until melted. Remove from heat

and stir in vanilla extract and a pinch of sea salt.

3. Pour the almond butter mixture over the dry ingredients and mix until well combined.

4. To make the mixture simpler to handle, refrigerate it for about half an hour.

5. Roll the mixture into bite-sized energy balls.

6. Store in the refrigerator and grab a couple of these dark chocolate and walnut energy bites as a delicious and brain-boosting snack.

These recipes showcase the incorporation of brain-boosting ingredients into enjoyable meals and snacks. Remember to maintain a balanced and varied diet, combining these recipes with other nutrient-rich foods to support overall brain health. Additionally, individual responses to these foods may vary, and it's always advisable to consult with a healthcare professional for personalized dietary recommendations.

Creating a brain-boosting dessert involves incorporating ingredients known for their cognitive benefits. Here's a recipe for a Blueberry and Dark Chocolate Chia Seed Pudding, combining the antioxidant-rich blueberries and dark chocolate with the omega-3 fatty acids from chia seeds:

Blueberry and Dark Chocolate Chia Seed Pudding:

Ingredients:

- 1/2 cup chia seeds
- 2 cups almond milk (or any milk of your choice)
- 1 teaspoon vanilla extract
- 2 tablespoons maple syrup or honey (adjust to taste)
- 1/2 cup fresh blueberries

- 2 tablespoons dark chocolate chips (70% cocoa or higher)
- Optional toppings: additional blueberries, chopped nuts, or a drizzle of dark chocolate

Instructions:

1. **Prepare the Chia Pudding Base:**
   - In a bowl, combine chia seeds, almond milk, vanilla extract, and maple syrup or honey. Make sure the chia seeds are dispersed evenly by giving it a good stir. To

avoid clumping, let it settle
for a few minutes and whisk
it once more.

2. **Refrigerate Overnight:**

    ○ Cover the bowl and
    refrigerate the chia pudding
    overnight or for at least 4
    hours. This enables the
    liquid to be absorbed by the
    chia seeds, giving the
    mixture a pudding-like
    consistency.

3. **Assemble the Dessert:**

    ○ Give the chia pudding a
    thorough stir when it has set.
    To get the right consistency,

thin it up with a little more

almond milk if it's too thick.

4. **Add Blueberries and Dark Chocolate:**

    o Gently fold in fresh blueberries and dark chocolate chips. The blueberries provide antioxidants, while dark chocolate contributes flavonoids that may support cognitive function.

5. **Serve and Garnish:**

    o Spoon the blueberry and dark chocolate chia pudding into individual serving bowls or glasses. Top with

additional blueberries,
chopped nuts, or a drizzle of
melted dark chocolate for
extra flair.

6. Enjoy Mindfully:

- Sit back, relax, and savor
  this brain-boosting dessert
  mindfully. The combination
  of chia seeds, blueberries,
  and dark chocolate offers a
  delightful treat that aligns
  with cognitive well-being.

7. Nutritional Benefits:

- Chia seeds are rich in omega-3 fatty acids, fiber, and antioxidants, supporting brain health by promoting proper neural communication and reducing oxidative stress. Almond milk provides essential nutrients and healthy fats, contributing to overall well-being.

8. Blueberries for Cognitive Function:

- Blueberries are often referred to as "brain berries" due to their high levels of anthocyanins, compounds that may improve

cognitive function. They have
been linked to benefits such as
better memory and concentration.

9. Dark Chocolate's Cognitive Boost:

- Dark chocolate, with its higher
cocoa content, contains flavonoids
that may enhance blood flow to
the brain. It has also been
connected to enhanced mood and
cognitive function.

10. Mindful Eating Practices:

- As you enjoy this brain-boosting dessert, practice mindful eating. Pay attention to the flavors, textures, and sensations. Mindful eating has been linked to improved overall well-being, including mental health.

11. Adaptations and Variations:

- Feel free to customize the recipe based on your preferences and dietary needs. You can experiment with different berries, use alternative sweeteners, or add a sprinkle of nuts for extra crunch and nutrients.

12. Share the Delight:

- Consider sharing this brain-boosting dessert with friends or family. Not only does it create a joyful experience, but sharing also fosters social connections, which contribute to cognitive well-being.

This dessert not only provides a delicious and satisfying treat but also incorporates ingredients with potential cognitive benefits. As always, moderation is key, and it's essential to complement such treats with an overall balanced and healthy diet.

Chapter three

Foods to eat to boost the brain

Consuming a well-balanced diet rich in nutrients is crucial for supporting brain health. Here are some foods that are considered beneficial for cognitive function and overall brain health:

1. **Fatty Fish:**

- Salmon, trout, and other fatty fish are excellent sources of omega-3 fatty acids, particularly DHA, which is crucial for brain health. Omega-3 fatty acids improve cognitive function and help

maintain the structural integrity of
brain cells.

2. Blueberries:

- Packed with antioxidants,
  blueberries help combat oxidative
  stress and inflammation,
  potentially reducing the risk of
  age-related cognitive decline.
  They are also linked to improved
  memory and cognitive
  performance.

3. Broccoli:

- Broccoli is rich in vitamin K and antioxidants, which help maintain a healthy brain. The formation of sphingolipids, a kind of fat that is tightly packed into brain cells, requires vitamin K.

4. Pumpkin Seeds:

- Rich in magnesium, iron, zinc, copper, and manganese, pumpkin seeds provide a variety of nutrients that support brain health. They also contain antioxidants and

a good amount of magnesium,
which is essential for learning and
memory.

5. Dark Chocolate:

- Dark chocolate with a cocoa
  content of 70% or higher contains
  flavonoids, caffeine, and
  antioxidants. These components
  may enhance memory and
  improve mood by increasing blood
  flow to the brain.

6. Nuts:

- Nuts high in antioxidants, vitamin E, and omega-3 fatty acids include walnuts and almonds. These nutrients contribute to overall brain health and may help reduce oxidative stress.

7. Eggs:

- Eggs are a good source of several nutrients, including choline, which is used to produce acetylcholine, a neurotransmitter important for mood and memory regulation.

8. Oranges:

- High in vitamin C, oranges and other citrus fruits help prevent mental decline. Vitamin C is a powerful antioxidant that protects the brain from damage caused by free radicals.

9. Turmeric:

- Turmeric's primary ingredient, curcumin, has antioxidant and anti-inflammatory properties. It may cross the blood-brain barrier and has been linked to potential improvements in memory and mood.

10. Avocado:

- Rich in monounsaturated fats, avocados contribute to healthy blood flow, which is crucial for maintaining optimal brain function. They also include folate, potassium, and vitamin K.

11. Whole Grains:

- Whole grains, such as quinoa, brown rice, and oats, provide a steady supply of energy to the brain. They release glucose slowly into the bloodstream, supporting sustained mental alertness.

12. Coffee:

- The caffeine in coffee acts as a natural stimulant, improving mood, alertness, and mental performance. It may also have long-term protective effects against cognitive decline.

Incorporating a variety of these foods into a balanced diet can contribute to overall brain health. It's important to note that no single food is a magic solution, and a holistic approach to nutrition, coupled with a healthy lifestyle, is key for optimal cognitive function.

Foods to avoid

While maintaining a healthy diet is essential for brain health, it's also beneficial to be aware of foods that may have a negative impact when consumed in excess. Here are some foods to consider moderating or avoiding for better cognitive health:

1. Sugary Foods and Beverages:

- High sugar intake, especially from sugary drinks and processed snacks, has been linked to cognitive decline and an increased risk of developing conditions like type 2 diabetes. Choose whole

fruits over sugary snacks.

2. Highly Processed Foods:

- Many processed foods contain additives, preservatives, and high levels of unhealthy fats. Diets high in processed foods have been associated with inflammation, which can negatively impact cognitive function.

3. Trans Fats:

- Found in some margarines, snack foods, and fried items, trans fats are known to contribute to inflammation and have been linked to an increased risk of cognitive decline.

4. High-Sodium Foods:

- Excessive salt intake can lead to high blood pressure, which may contribute to cognitive decline over time. Limit intake of processed

and salty foods, and focus on a
diet rich in fresh, whole foods.

5. Excessive Alcohol:

- While moderate alcohol
  consumption may have some
  cardiovascular benefits, excessive
  alcohol intake can lead to
  cognitive impairment, memory
  loss, and an increased risk of
  neurodegenerative disorders.

6. Saturated Fats:

- Foods high in saturated fats, such as red meat and full-fat dairy products, should be consumed in moderation. Diets rich in saturated fats have been associated with an increased risk of cognitive decline.

7. Artificial Sweeteners:

- Some studies suggest that artificial sweeteners, found in diet sodas and sugar-free products, may have negative effects on gut bacteria, potentially impacting cognitive health. Opt for natural sweeteners in moderation.

8. White Bread and Refined Grains:

- Refined grains, like those found in white bread and certain cereals, lack the nutrients and fiber found in whole grains. Diets high in refined carbohydrates may lead to blood sugar spikes and negatively impact cognitive function.

9. Fried Foods:

- Foods that are deep-fried or
  cooked at high temperatures may
  contain unhealthy trans fats and
  can contribute to oxidative stress,
  potentially harming brain cells.

10. Processed Meats:

- Processed meats like sausages,
bacon, and deli meats often contain high
levels of sodium and saturated fats.
Diets rich in processed meats have
been associated with an increased risk
of cognitive decline.

11. High-Mercury Fish:

- While fatty fish are generally beneficial, some types of fish, like shark, swordfish, and king mackerel, can contain high levels of mercury, which may have adverse effects on the nervous system. Go for fish that has less mercury, such as salmon, trout, and sardines.

12. High-Caffeine Energy Drinks:

- While moderate caffeine consumption can have cognitive benefits, excessive intake from energy drinks may lead to negative effects such as increased anxiety and disrupted sleep patterns.

Remember that moderation and balance are key. It's always a good idea to consult with a healthcare professional or a registered dietitian for personalized dietary advice based on individual health needs and conditions.

Chapter four

Supplements for brain booster

While it's essential to obtain most nutrients from a well-balanced diet, certain supplements may be considered to support brain health. It's crucial to note that individual responses to supplements can vary, and it's advisable to consult with a healthcare professional before adding any new supplements to your routine. Here are some supplements that are commonly associated with potential cognitive benefits:

1. Omega-3 Fatty Acids:

- Source: Fish oil supplements (EPA and DHA).
- Benefits: Supports brain structure and function, potentially aiding in memory and cognitive performance.

2. Vitamin B Complex:

- Source: B-vitamin supplements or a combination of B-vitamins (B6, B9, B12).
- Benefits: Essential for cognitive development and function, helps

regulate homocysteine levels

linked to cognitive decline.

3. Vitamin D:

- Source: Vitamin D supplements.

- Benefits: Supports overall brain

  health, and deficiencies have been

  linked to cognitive impairment.

4. Magnesium:

- Source: Magnesium supplements.

- Benefits: Plays a role in

  neuroplasticity, synaptic function,

and may have a calming effect on
the brain.

5. Acetyl-L-Carnitine:

- Source: Acetyl-L-carnitine
  supplements.
- Benefits: May enhance
  mitochondrial function, supporting
  energy production in brain cells.

6. Ginkgo Biloba:

- Source: Ginkgo biloba
  supplements.

- Benefits: May improve blood flow to the brain and have antioxidant properties, potentially supporting cognitive function.

7. Bacopa Monnieri:

- Source: Bacopa monnieri supplements.
- Benefits: Traditionally used in Ayurvedic medicine, it may have cognitive-enhancing effects and promote memory.

8. Curcumin (Turmeric Extract):

- Source: Curcumin supplements or turmeric extracts.
- Benefits: Known for its anti-inflammatory and antioxidant properties, may have neuroprotective effects.

9. Phosphatidylserine:

- Source: Phosphatidylserine supplements.
- Benefits: A component of cell membranes, it may support

cognitive function, especially in memory.

10. Rhodiola Rosea:

- Source: Rhodiola rosea supplements.

- Benefits: An adaptogenic herb, it may help combat stress and fatigue, potentially supporting cognitive performance.

11. Coenzyme Q10 (CoQ10):

- Source: CoQ10 supplements.

- Benefits: Important for mitochondrial function, it has antioxidant properties and may support overall brain health.

12. Caffeine:

- Source: Caffeine supplements or from natural sources like coffee or tea.

- Benefits: Known for its stimulating effects, caffeine can enhance alertness, mood, and cognitive performance.

Note: It's crucial to be cautious with supplement dosage and potential interactions with medications or other supplements. Pregnant or nursing individuals, as well as those with pre-existing health conditions, should consult with a healthcare professional before taking supplements.

Always prioritize a well-balanced diet, regular exercise, sufficient sleep, and stress management for optimal brain health. Supplements need to support a healthy lifestyle—not take its place.

How to build the brain muscle

Building "brain muscle" is a metaphorical way to describe enhancing cognitive abilities, improving mental resilience, and optimizing brain function. Here are several lifestyle practices and activities that can contribute to building a strong and resilient brain:

1. Mental Stimulation:

- Engage in intellectually challenging activities such as puzzles, crosswords, chess, or learning a new instrument. These activities stimulate different parts of the brain and promote neural plasticity.

2. Lifelong Learning:

- Embrace a mindset of continuous learning. Read books, take courses, or acquire new skills regularly. Learning new things

helps create new neural
connections and keeps the brain
active.

3. Physical Exercise:

- Regular aerobic exercise has
  been linked to improved cognitive
  function and increased
  neuroplasticity. Try to get in at
  least 150 minutes a week of
  moderate-to-intense activity.

4. Balanced Diet:

- Consume a nutrient-rich diet with a focus on whole foods, including fruits, vegetables, whole grains, lean proteins, and healthy fats. Vitamins, antioxidants, and omega-3 fatty acids are very good for the brain.

5. Quality Sleep:

- Getting enough good sleep is top priority. Sleep is essential for maintaining memory, thinking clearly, and the general health of the brain.

6. Stress Management:

- Engage in stress-relieving activities like yoga, deep breathing exercises, or mindfulness meditation. Chronic stress can negatively impact the brain, so finding effective stress management strategies is essential.

7. Social Connections:

- Maintain strong social connections and engage in meaningful social interactions. Socializing can provide emotional support, reduce stress, and contribute to cognitive well-being.

8. Stay Hydrated:

- Proper hydration is essential for optimal brain function. Dehydration can lead to cognitive fatigue and impaired concentration.

9. Mindfulness and Meditation:

- Incorporate mindfulness practices and meditation into your routine. Mindfulness can improve attention, focus, and overall cognitive performance.

10. Set Goals and Stay Motivated:

- Establish clear goals for personal and professional development. Having goals provides a sense of purpose and motivation, stimulating the brain to stay active and engaged.

11. Novel Experiences:

- Step out of your comfort zone and seek new experiences. Whether it's trying a new hobby, traveling to unfamiliar places, or meeting new people, novelty stimulates the brain and promotes adaptability.

12. Cognitive Training Apps:

- Utilize brain-training apps that offer exercises designed to enhance memory, attention, and problem-solving skills. While not a substitute for a well-rounded lifestyle, these apps can provide additional mental stimulation.

Remember that building and maintaining a strong "brain muscle" involves a combination of these practices. Just as physical exercise is crucial for building muscle strength, a holistic approach to mental well-being contributes to cognitive vitality and resilience.

Consistency and a commitment to a

healthy lifestyle are key elements in

nurturing a strong and adaptable brain.

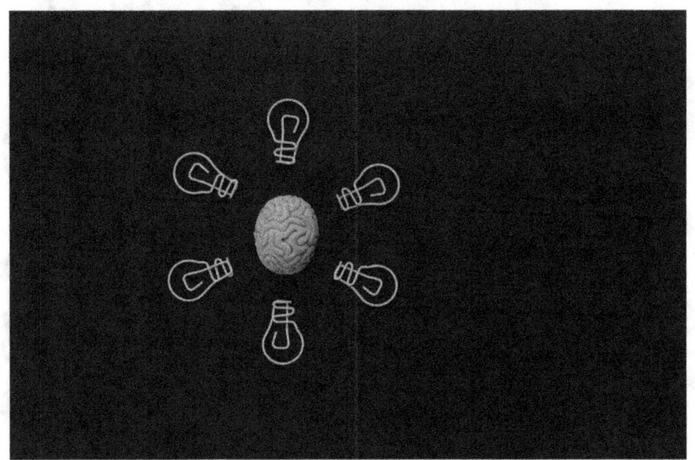

Chapter five

A 30 day meal plan for brain boosting

Sure, here's a sample 30-day meal plan focused on brain-boosting foods:

Day 1-10:

1. Breakfast: Oatmeal with berries and nuts.
2. Snack: Greek yogurt with honey and walnuts.
3. Lunch: Salmon salad with leafy greens and avocado.

4. Snack: Carrot and celery sticks with hummus.

5. Dinner: Quinoa bowl with spinach, tomatoes, and grilled chicken.

Day 11-20:

1. Breakfast consists of poached eggs and avocado over whole grain bread.

2. Snack: Blueberries and almonds.

3. Lunch: Lentil soup with a side of mixed vegetables.

4. Snack: Dark chocolate and a small apple.

5. Dinner: Baked sweet potato with broccoli and grilled fish.

Day 21-30:

1. Breakfast: Smoothie with spinach, banana, and berries.
2. Snack: Cottage cheese with pineapple.
3. Lunch: Quinoa salad with chickpeas, cucumber, and feta cheese.
4. Snack: Mixed nuts and dried fruits.
5. Dinner: Stir-fried tofu with broccoli and brown rice.

Remember to stay hydrated throughout
the day with water, herbal teas, and
incorporate omega-3 fatty acids,
antioxidants, and a variety of colorful
fruits and vegetables for optimal brain
health. Adjust portion sizes based on
your individual needs and consult a
nutritionist for personalized advice.

Conclusion

In conclusion, the landscape of brain boosters is marked by a diverse array of approaches, ranging from nutritional supplements and nootropics to lifestyle modifications and cognitive exercises. While the allure of enhancing cognitive function is undeniable, it is crucial to approach these interventions with a balanced perspective, considering both the potential benefits and the limitations.

The market is saturated with various products claiming to boost brain function, each accompanied by bold promises and optimistic testimonials.

However, it is imperative to navigate this terrain with a critical mindset, as the scientific evidence supporting the efficacy and safety of many brain boosters remains inconclusive. Rigorous research and clinical trials are essential to establish the true potential and risks associated with these interventions.

One of the key takeaways from the existing body of knowledge is the importance of lifestyle factors in influencing cognitive health. Regular exercise, proper nutrition, sufficient sleep, and stress management contribute significantly to overall brain function. These foundational elements should not be overlooked in the pursuit of quick-fix solutions or magic pills.

Nutritional supplements, such as omega-3 fatty acids, antioxidants, and vitamins, have been implicated in supporting cognitive health. However, the supplementation landscape is complex, with individual responses varying widely. Striking a balance between obtaining essential nutrients from a well-rounded diet and considering targeted supplementation may be a prudent approach.

Nootropics, substances specifically designed to enhance cognitive function,

have gained popularity. However, the
regulatory framework surrounding these
compounds is often lax, and their
long-term safety remains a subject of
debate. Responsible usage, informed by
scientific evidence, is paramount to
mitigate potential risks and unintended
consequences.

The individuality of cognitive function
must also be acknowledged. It's
possible that what works for one
individual won't always benefit another.
Genetic factors, baseline cognitive
abilities, and overall health contribute to
the variability in responses to brain
boosters. Personalized approaches,

guided by professional advice, may be more effective in optimizing cognitive performance.

Ethical considerations loom large in the pursuit of brain boosters, particularly when it comes to pharmaceutical interventions. The distinction between enhancement and augmentation raises ethical dilemmas, and the potential societal implications of widespread cognitive enhancement should be carefully considered.

In essence, the quest for brain boosters is a nuanced journey that demands a comprehensive understanding of the interplay between lifestyle, nutrition, and cognitive function. While the allure of quick fixes persists, a holistic and evidence-based approach remains the most reliable path toward achieving and maintaining optimal brain health. As the scientific community continues to unravel the intricacies of the brain, a cautious and informed perspective will be instrumental in navigating the evolving landscape of cognitive enhancement.